Fashion Photography

8 Practical Fashion Photography Tips For Your Models to Shine

James Carren

© 2015 Sender Publishing

For more books by this author, please visit
www.photographybooks.us

Table of Contents

Introduction

Fashion photography is one of my favorite genres, and also one of the most complex. I think that it is unique in that it requires the help of a talented team of people in order to pull it off. Fashion isn't something that you can do alone. It is also a genre that is incredibly work intensive, from conception to finish. If you have an eye for fashion, and you have never done a fashion shoot before, then you're probably very enamored by the idea. I know I was. If you're an experienced fashion photographer, then you know how fulfilling, and how work intensive such a shoot can be.

My goal with this book is to explain each step in the process of a fashion shoot, and thus help you pull your first one off with less hitches than you otherwise would have had. (Trust me, no matter how well prepared you are, there will always be a hitch. It's just the nature of the beast). If you are an experienced photographer, then my goal is to perhaps give you a new idea or two on how to do things.

First off, I want to break down and explore the different types of fashion photography. There is no way to cover them all, but by giving an overview, I hope to be able to give you some ideas of something you might want to explore. Who knows, you may find your niche aesthetic, or you may find something with which to expand your portfolio.

Secondly, I want to explain the difference between portraiture and fashion photography. While they do overlap, they are definitely two completely separate genres. I feel that that is important to make clear, because you should make sure that your intent is a fashion shoot before you begin.

A huge chunk of the book is going to be focused on how to make your shoot run smoothly and successfully. From the very

1

beginning, you have to be fully invested and clear in what you want to achieve. This is incredibly important because you will be working with so many other people, and you want to be on the same page and appear put together and professional, even if you don't necessarily feel that way. I'll introduce the members you should have on your team, and tell you step by step how to keep them informed. I'll also talk a little bit about photo shoot etiquette, which applies both to you and your team, as well as the models you'll work with.

There will be a section on shooting on location and in the studio. I'll go through how they differ and how to set up and prepare for each. I'll suggest a checklist of items you may need in either situation, and talk about some lighting styles mentioned in the section on fashion photography aesthetics.

Everyone alive today knows that retouching is a huge and controversial subject when it comes to the world of fashion. I want to touch on a little bit of the politics of the matter, because I feel that it's important that every fashion photographer come to terms with where they stand on the subject, and what instances they feel retouching is appropriate. Basic retouching techniques will be discussed, as well as some more advanced techniques for things like skin smoothing, hair removal, brightening and slimming of a model.

Your portfolio is what you show the world, and whether it's online, in print, or both, it's how you make your voice heard and land jobs. Organization is very important because you want it to flow well and be impressive at start and finish. You want to leave your client or juror with a lasting and strong impression. While diversity in a portfolio is important in some respects, you also want your aesthetic to remain unified and strong, and you don't want to really come off as a jack of all trades, because that isn't interesting or unique.

And finally, I want to leave you with a small section on print for fashion, which is vastly different from print for fine art genres. There is an industry standard, and while you don't necessarily have to abide by it for a portfolio, it tends to make it undoubtedly clear that you intend that concept for a fashion publication. Graphics are also incredibly important when it comes to fashion, because at the end of the day, fashion is a subset of the advertising world.

Overall, I hope that this book is a good exposure to the world of fashion photography and that it helps you in your journey to make photographs in this genre.

What's the Difference Between Portraiture and Fashion Photography?

In my career as a photographer, I often find that people are confused about the differences between portraiture and fashion photography. Before we get started on the types of fashion photography and how to go about being the successful fashion photographer, I feel that we should define the difference so that you can make sure of what you're trying to achieve.

The reason that portraiture and fashion photography often get confused is because they both rely heavily on the use of people. However it should be made clear immediately that portraiture is about the identity personality of the sitter, whereas fashion is a glamorized marketing campaign. While the look of the person in the fashion campaign matters from the perspective of what is being projected, the identity and personality of the person is not the focus. The person merely is there to be vehicle for the clothing or accessories.

With portraiture, photographers shoot people who are from all walks of life. Generally, they don't try to change the person even if the image is posed. For a fashion model, the image is all about becoming the paragon of what that fashion line is. The girl could become anyone that she has never been before in her life. In essence, the fashion model is an actress or actor, whereas the portrait sitter is all about capturing that moment of truth.

Now, that is not to say that you don't want fashion models with attitude, because that is definitely a must. Especially in high fashion, the model must be willing to take on an exaggerated persona, and have the confidence to carry off often ridiculous looks.

Fashion photography is often very cutting edge and can be seen as artwork as well. It's all about pushing boundaries and making the ridiculous beautiful. There's also this misconception that fashion photography has to be hollow and shallow, but in truth, a lot of fashion photography also falls into the realm of conceptual photography. With fashion, you have the license to say whatever it is that you need to say. The clothes remain the main element, but they can often provide elegant mask for political or personal statement. This is what makes fashion photography so important. It's part of our everyday lives because it really is just beautiful advertising. But what can you also advertise along with the clothes?

Fashion Photography Types and Styles

Now that you have the definition of fashion photography, it's probably a bit easier to identify. However it is important to note that there are thousands upon thousands of styles a fashion photographer can have. So what's the difference between a fashion photography type and a fashion photography style? This is what I'm going to define for you here. A type of fashion photography falls along the lines of things like: lifestyle, beauty, editorial, (which also has a subset of haute couture) and straight up advertising. These are the five main genres I will be focusing on.

Style is different from type in that it is unique to every photographer. A photographer can be a beauty photographer who is happy and bright, or they can be moody and dark. It's all up to personal preference. So let's get started talking about the different types.

Lifestyle

I've got to tell you, lifestyle tends to be my least favorite style of fashion photography. Lifestyle also tends to be the only photography type that has one consistent style: happy and overly cheerful. It's generally marketed towards teenage girls and you'll see it in magazines such as Teen Vogue and Elle Girl. So what defines lifestyle photography? Well, often you'll see adolescent boys and girls happy and smiling, engaging in some posed activity. They could be on the beach, camping, at a football game, playing with a dog, or any other fun and conceivably carefree activity. It's light, and often has no conceptual thought behind it other than what you see directly before you. Also, it tends to stick with bright colors and lots of sunlight.

Recently, companies such as Urban Outfitters and Aerie have tried to redefine lifestyle photography. They still stick with young teenagers, but instead of everything being light and bubbly and overly bright, they've gone with the sun soaked bohemian look. This style is very popular on Instagram and Tumblr, and then you'll see lots of long, blonde hair, fields of flowers or wheat fields, and light leaks.

Beauty

Beauty is the style that for me, most closely rides the line between portraiture and fashion photography. Beauty is typically and technically of portrait. However, it remains in the realm of fashion photography because the portrait is not about the personality of the person sitting for it. Instead, the main focus of the beauty portrait is going to be either hair, makeup, or accessories. In this way, beauty is an elevated advertising campaign. It's also consistently smooth unlike portraits, which serve to capture imperfections.

Editorial

So, just as a disclaimer, editorial can be an ad and an ad can be an editorial. In that case, what's the difference between the two? Editorials are what you see in high-end magazines, whereas ads are marketed toward a specific audience for a specific product. While editorial can advertise something such as a Famous fashion designer or a luxury jewelry brand, it's about the art, the edginess, and the vision of the photographer and creative director. Lighting will be much darker and moodier, and you might also have an artistic or political statement behind the image. Think Prada versus Target.

An editorial can also be the specific artistic vision of a particular photographer. They have a concept they want to shoot, they have designers they would like to use, and they're so well-known that they get asked by magazines to shoot for them.

Haute Couture

I like to think of haute couture as an editorial on steroids. Haute couture is not necessarily an ad because most people would never be able to afford those clothes. Instead, the clothes have been elevated to a pure art form. Look for is the most exquisite form of fashion photography and often the most ridiculous. It's pure concept, pure statement, and pure fantasy. It can often be edgy and disturbing, and is also often found on gallery walls as well as magazine pages.

Advertising

Advertising, as I said before, is all about targeting and marketing to a very specific audience. While an editorial can be advertising it does not always have to be, and typically, advertising is much cleaner and simpler aesthetic. It's bright, it's pretty, and it's clean so that there is room for the advertising copy.

Organizing Your Shoot

One of the most important things you can do on a fashion shoot is to be organized. Organization is key to any photo shoot, but I feel that it reaches a new level of importance when fashion is involved. This is because fashion is definitely not an industry in which you can work solo…you need a team of other trusted people to help you carry it off. If you as the photographer are not prepared, it can look really bad, especially since if you are self-directing, then you are the head of your team. And if you aren't self-directing, then you cost your boss and your team a lot of money and time when you aren't well prepared.

For this chapter, I'm going to be working under the assumption that you are in charge of your own shoot and walk you through how to set up a team and be prepared for anything that might come your way.

First on your team is yourself: the photographer. You may also want to have an assistant there, whether it's to help with equipment setup or just to be another set of eyes on the lookout for anything funky. What I typically do is have my assistant sit next to the monitor (that is, if you are shooting tethered) and watch as the images come up on the screen. This can help to prevent a myriad of problems and save everyone involved a lot of time. Have the assistant watch out for any technical issues, such as lighting that needs to be adjusted, as well as hair and clothing detail and the model's pose. Have them tell you if a pose looks awkward or if the framing needs to be adjusted in any way. Of course, you should always walk over and check up on your own pictures as well, but over time, if you use the same assistant, they should develop a repertoire with you and an eye for your style, which is helpful.

9

Next, you need your stylist. Now, some photographers, like myself, do like to style their own shoots. But if you aren't doing it yourself, having a stylist is key for fashion. You should first have a discussion with your stylist so that they know specifically what it is that you want. It might be good to show them some inspiration photos for the style you are looking for. Using platforms such as Tumblr, Instagram, Pinterest, and Polyvore are a huge help. I find that I like Pinterest and Polyvore the most as a finished product because their final layout is reminiscent of a mood board. After your mood board has been created, it's easy to print it out and show it to the members of your team so that everyone has an accurate visual of the end goal.

After drawing up the mood board, you might want to go out shopping with your stylist, although again, if you have developed an excellent repoire, then they can probably do it alone. Make sure you always allocate a budget, and do research around your area to see if there are any vintage stores or costume shops that rent garments, because that's often much cheaper than outright purchasing. You might also look into sites such as Rent the Runway, and take a trip to your local thrift store (Goodwill, Salvation Army or anything local) for cheap but cool finds and basics.

If you have a designer that you're working with on the shoot, I find that it can be a mixed bag allowing them on set, so it's really just up to personal preference and necessity. If you're just doing basic product shots, you might not want them there, but if they have a specific aesthetic they want you to achieve, they should also participate in the making of mood boards and shopping for items that compliment theirs. Having them on set can also be extremely helpful to your stylist, especially with regards to how the garments should lay.

Next, you need a hairstylist and a makeup artist, or MUA. Both of these team members should remain on set for the entirety of the shoot. While it is the responsibility of the photographer and of the assistant to make sure hair and makeup stay in place, the hairstylist and MUA should be able to do touchups at any point. If you're going to be working with a particularly elaborate hair or makeups style, make sure you send them reference materials. This gives them a clear visual as well as the chance to practice the style beforehand and make sure they have all the proper materials.

This is the absolute minimum you need for a successful fashion team, although I would also suggest having a seamstress on set. This isn't necessary if you're working with a seasoned fashion designer.

Let's move on to talking about models. Fashion photography is all about the image that you want the clothes or accessories to project. It's important that you ask your designer (or yourself, as the case may be), what kind of image you're looking for, because that's really going to inform the kind of model you pick. There is always the traditional model type, whom you can hire from any local booking agency. Just look to see what agencies you have available in your town. You might be looking for alternative models, or it's also possible to use friends if they have the experience. As you find models you like, you should keep a book with all their stats (height, weight, hair color, tattoos, willing to dye hair, willing to be nude) and current contact information as well as rates. That way, when you have a shoot coming up, you have references you can show your client if they don't know quite what they want, and you aren't scrambling for a phone number.

If you're going to be working with professional models, they'll be sure to show up, but you'll also have to pay them. You should definitely come up with a budget for what you can afford. If you don't have the money to pay a model, then you might have to work with people who aren't professional. This is perfectly fine, but it might take a little bit longer to get what you want. In either case, you should always compensate your models and your team in some way for their time and effort, even if all you can do is feed them or buy them coffee.

If there's one thing I've learned when not working with professional models, it's that you should have several backups. Models are notorious for being late and for canceling at the last minute. Make sure you are constantly communicating with your primary model and also with the backups. You might also think about instating a call time that is actually earlier than the beginning of the shoot. That way, you give yourself some leeway for everyone to get there on time.

Try to get your models into hair and makeup as you and your assistant are setting up for the shoot. This saves everyone time and everyone tends to be ready around the same time. And you never want to send them to hair and makeup in the fashion you'll be shooting. If you do, you run the risk of staining the garment, which only creates more work for you in post.

Now, let's talk toolkits. You always, always, always want to have a toolkit with you at any shoot. If you think you might need it, you probably will the second you don't have it. Everyone's toolkit varies a little bit based on the needs of a shoot and what your habits are. Along with things like a hammer, nails, and a screwdriver, you'll want to pack things like: emergency film, duct tape, fashion tape, shoe inserts, chicken cutlets (breast inserts) a needle and thread, hook and eyes, and a small first aid kit. I would suggest making yourself a checklist of anything you think you might need and making sure you've got it all at least the night before. This is also a good idea to get into with your camera equipment.

Finally, in order to get your shoot going smoothly, you'll want to develop a good working relationship with your models, which should make them feel at ease with you. You still want to maintain a professional demeanor, but being friendly, encouraging, explanatory and firm is always a huge help. Modeling can make some people feel very uncomfortable because they feel that they might make a fool of themselves, so it's important that you also be willing to make yourself look silly. Don't be afraid to demonstrate a pose if they are struggling.

If they feel that what they are doing is over the top and don't understand why it has to be so exaggerated, just explain to them that it has to translate on camera for the sake of the concept. It might even help to allow them to see a really good shot, which will build their confidence. I also find that speaking with your models before a shoot helps build trust...they are more willing to listen to you if they feel that you are comfortable to be around but also in control. Low music during a shoot is also a good idea; it helps the model get into a zone especially if the music exudes the kind of mood you are trying to capture.

With all these tips in place, you should be well on your way to having a successful, smooth shoot. Just be sure to be in open and full communication with all the members of your team, and be very clear and firm about what you want during all steps in the process. If you're like me, then making checklists is going to be huge to you. They help keep you organized and ensure that you don't forget anything. You might even want to save a template in Word and print it out before every shoot, so that you have a standardized checklist with you as you prepare.

Shooting On Location

I have to say, my absolute favorite method of shooting is shooting on location. It's great because it gets you out of the studio, into the sun, or into a really cool interior. If you've decided that you would like to shoot on location for a fashion shoot, you should make plans to go to location scouting. When you do your mood board, don't just include Fashion and makeup looks you would like. Also include images of the kind of vibe you're going for and the kind of location you would like to shoot at. Do some research around your area for a similar location, but be prepared to drive to it as well. This is part of why you want to make sure you're as well prepared for your shoot as you can be. Once you go on location, if you've left anything behind then you just have to go without it.

You also go location scouting to make sure that a prospective location is absolutely what you want, or can be made that way. The last thing you want is to rely on someone else's pictures of location, and then get there and find that's not what you're looking for. Always take the time to familiarize yourself with the lay of the land, or the layout of the building you are using. You want to know where you're shooting and an idea of what the end result will look like.

If the place you want to shoot is someone else's private property, you should always get in touch with them and ask them whether it's okay to shoot there. Some public places that allow you to book time will require a fee or a permit of some sort. When you shoot without a permit you run the risk of being asked to leave before you're finished, or worse, potentially being in legal trouble.

Now that we've got etiquette out of the way, let's talk about how to harness natural light when you're shooting outside. Always try to shoot during a time of the day that has the most pleasing and even light. This would be the golden hour, or just as the sun is coming up or going down. You never, ever want to shoot in the middle of the day, because that's when shadows are long and harsh. If you do have to shoot at such time, you should look for open shade, such as comes from a tree or the overhang of the building. Try to use it along with reflectors to balance out the light. A lot of people are under the misconception that the best light for fashion is bright sun. Now, if you're doing a lifestyle piece where you want a lot of light leaks, then bright sun coming into your photograph is probably something you want. However for most other styles, the best light you could have is actually that of an overcast day. If it's necessary that you have the sky in the shot, you can always shoot a nice blue sky on another day and Photoshop it in post.

If you want to use lights on location in order to fully control what it looks like, you can get a generator into which to plug your lights. These can be ordered for rent at any of your local photo shops.

Shooting In Studio

Shooting in studio is the most complex setup you can choose. However, it does make for a very clean image that is good for advertising copy. Rather than going through lighting setups, which I believe reading without a visual can be very confusing, I just want to talk to you about the types of lights and light modifiers you would use in fashion.

Let's start with lights. Hot lights are what I first began shooting with, but they are typically tungsten, which can have a bit of a green tinge to it. They are also relatively inexpensive, but as the name suggests, very hot, so you'll only want to use them for short periods of time. They're also great because, unlike monolights and power packs, they allow you to see what the light will look like accurately before you take the picture.

Monolights are an all in one light that kind of works like a power pack but is much more portable and convenient, although not as powerful.

Then you have power packs, which are a strobe, not a continuous light. Power packs can be set to different amounts of power, so that you can control how bright it is. Also, you control how long the flash goes off. And power packs can support more than one light, so you can do a two or three light setup off one power pack depending on the model you have. Just for reference, I have always used Profoto products and find them to be of very high quality.

Next we have light modifiers. Light modifiers are anything that you use to control how the light falls on your subject. This includes things like umbrellas, traditional softboxes, octoboxes, and strip boxes. You can also use a parabolic umbrella, however, I find that most of the time it's really not necessary, and you can do just as much with a plain old umbrella. Now, you also have beauty dishes, which, as the name suggests, are commonly used for beauty and fashion shots. So what do all these things do? Essentially, they are light diffusers that make the light more even and pleasing across the field. Umbrellas, when placed over the subject's head off to the side bounce light onto the face. Softboxes, octoboxes, and strip boxes work much the same as cloud cover on an overcast day. They make the light much more even and mild across the area they cover. I prefer octoboxes because they are rounder and larger in shape, although strip lighting can be good to highlight things like jewelry. Speaking of which, if you are doing a jewelry shoot, you might want to make use of a modifier called a snoot, which is a small cone-shaped apparatus that you affix over a light in order to narrow it and constrain it on one small area. Beauty dishes are also light diffusers, but the look is much harsher, which is good for bringing out high cheekbones in fashion shoots. They look especially good when the model is wearing a large amount of makeup. Because they are harsher, they're also good for lighting male models, whose bone structure can take more contrast.

Lighting setups, I've found, are largely discovered by experimentation. Of course you do want to remember that the face is important, and needs to be lit by a main light and a hair light. You might also choose to use a backdrop light as well, although it really just depends on how complex you want to get and how much equipment you have at your disposal.

Before you begin to shoot, it's always a good idea to do a couple of test shots. Have your model standing about the same places she will be for most of the shots, and make sure that your hair light, main light, and backdrop light are all at an appropriate height and distance. Then set up any extra lights you might have for details on the clothing or accessories. As you discover lighting techniques that you like, I would suggest writing them down in a notebook that you keep solely for this purpose. That way when you do similar shoots in the future, you can easily flip through and refer to the lighting setups you did before. If you're shooting film, also keep track of the type, ISO, and aperture and shutter speed. This will help your shoot to run much more quickly and smoothly. Plus, writing things down helps you to remember them, so over time you will be able to recall your favorite lighting setups from memory.

Retouching For Fashion

Retouching is, and always has been necessary to the fashion industry, and to the photo industry as well. Retouching is not inherently good or bad, however it has gained a reputation for being excessive and damaging to the psyches of young women. Therefore, at the beginning of this, I would like to make a very clear distinction between retouching to make a photo look it's best, and retouching to completely alter a photograph. Both undoubtedly have a place in the realm of fashion photography, it's just a question of morality and ethics that determine how it is used.

Retouching can be used as a tool to bring out the existing natural beauty of a model. It can also be used to make a model look like a completely different person. Is it ethical to do this? Of course everyone is going to have their own opinion, but I feel that in some instances it can be beneficial. Such instances include: fantasy photographs in which the model is made to look like an otherworldly creature, and political discourse on the subject of retouching i.e. overly Photoshopped photos that makes the models look anorexic as a statement against the overuse of retouching. I think personally that retouching is unethical when used to an extreme in fashion marketing campaigns. Not only does it make the actual model feel more pressure to be even thinner than she already is, but the message that we send to young girls is that the only way to be beautiful is to be "fashionably thin." This is inherently damaging to girls who are not naturally thin, and even to girls who are, who they believe they should be thinner.

So how can we use retouching ethically? Well, my first tip is going to be to use it as a tool to enhance the natural beauty of a model. Get rid of any acne or marks that wouldn't be flattering on anyone, and remove any redness or blotchiness from the skin. Even if you have decided to move forward with more advanced retouching techniques, this is always where you want to start. Follow up blemish and redness removal with a general skin smoothing. Fashion photography tends to look a little glossier than other types of pictures, so it's okay if you do a little bit more than you typically would on a portrait. However, you still want to make sure that the skin has some texture to it, because you don't want your model looking like a droid. I would suggest doing the smoothing by using the high pass filter, and then bringing some texture back in with a brush on another layer. You'll also want to use the high pass to up the detail in her eyes, eyelashes, and lips. Also make sure that you never smooth the texture out of hair.

Following that, you want to do any necessary cleanup to the image. This includes things like removing flyaway or stray hairs, cleaning up and/or arching eyebrows, and ensuring that clothing doesn't have any unwanted wrinkling. If your model is wearing something like a graphic tee, you might also want to consider replacing or sharpening the lettering so that it can be clearly read.

After this step, is when retouching tends to get a bit questionable for me, because we get into the face and body slimming. Now, if you have a tiny bit of love handle that the model or client isn't a fan of and wants you to tuck in, go for it. However, I personally draw the line at complete slimming or body reshaping unless you have a solid artistic reason. Also, using the liquify mesh can be extremely difficult until you've had lots of practice, so if you want to use it, I would suggest practicing on a test shot before you try to tackle an otherwise finished shot.

And no matter what, always remember to use layers and practice nondestructive editing. It's good to have a before and after portfolio if you want to get retouching jobs, plus it's always good to have an original master copy in case you ever need to re-edit.

Organizing Your Portfolio

After the actual creation of photographs, I feel that the portfolio is the next most important component for any photographer. How you put your portfolio together is either going to make or break you to clients or jurors. Unfortunately, I feel that many photographers underestimate the power of the portfolio. In fact, I am consistently shocked at the amount of artists and photographers that I know who don't have a website, and who put all of their work indiscriminately together. This is an incredibly bad practice to get into. Firstly, you really need to have both a print portfolio and an online presence. If you cannot afford a domain name or your own website, you should at least maintain a Facebook page. Now, in that case Facebook pages work a little bit differently than normal websites. Because of the nature of the Facebook page, you probably will not delete older work which no longer applies to your aesthetic. However, with a traditional website, you should go through it every few months and add new work. You then either have the option of deleting old work, or of archiving it, which is my personal choice. I find that it reminds me of where I came from and that my clients enjoy seeing the change in my work.

Considering the fact that we live in a digital age, many people feel that they no longer need a print portfolio. While it is completely valid to have your work solely online, and to bring in a laptop or iPod on which to show it, photographic work loses something when you can't see it on a piece of paper that you can actually touch. Paper is so versatile, and it brings in another tactile element to your image. You have the option of texture or smoothness, of glossy or matte, of metallic, or any color you might imagine. It also allows you to show off another skill set, which is that of printing. Printing is an art form which must be done correctly in order to fully showcase an image. Print or digital aside, it's important that you organize your portfolio in such a way that it flows well and is impressive. Also, you might want to consider making your physical print portfolio much smaller than your online portfolio. This is because typically, when a client or juror looks at print portfolio, they only take about ten minutes to do so. You don't want to overwhelm them with too many images that are not strong enough or important enough to you. Typically, I limit myself to approximately 21 images. You'll also want to group your images for convenience, whether this be by genre if you shoot singular photographs, or by series if you shoot in format. Because you are limited to so few images, You might either choose to show only one or two series, or to show the strongest images that can stand on their own from several series. So how do you go about organizing a portfolio? You always want to put your strongest foot forward, and end with your strongest foot forward. That is not to say that the images in the middle of the portfolio should be weak, but they would be the "weakest" of the bunch, unless you are going chronologically for a series. Being a visual person, I find that the easiest way for me to determine where an image should go in a portfolio is to go ahead and make prints of my prospective ones, (if I'm unsure of the images I want to use, I'll narrow it down to about 25 or 30 images and go from there) and lay them out on the floor to rearrange them until I am satisfied with their order.

As you're doing this, you should consider what images you feel truly speak to who you are as a photographer. Don't be afraid to be brutal with yourself. If you allow yourself to hang onto a photograph due to the sentimental value that might hold for you, you run the risk of making your portfolio weaker. Consider the content, and what kind of statement you're trying to make with your images. Also consider the technical proficiency of each image. Is the exposure good? Is it too dark or too blown out in any place? Is it balanced and dynamic, or static and boring? Consider your photography from all angles; you know what it means to you, but other people might see it differently. If you are concerned about your points not coming across as you wish them to, have some friends and fellow photographers take a look and give you feedback before you make your final decision. The editing process may only take you hours or it may take you weeks, so be sure to give yourself plenty of time. I would also suggest not including the work that is older than about three years. You want your portfolio to stay updated and relevant to who you are today, not where you came from. Remember to take any constructive criticism you might get with a grain of salt; while it is important to listen and take note, at the end of the day the final decision is yours. If you feel very strongly about an image, hang on to it even if others don't like it because who knows? It might actually be your strongest and most impressive piece.

Before closing out this chapter, I also want to talk about portfolio diversification. Many new and untrained photographers believe that the more skill sets you can show, the better. While you do want to show that you're technically proficient, I feel that at the level of having your portfolio critiqued, this should be given. You don't need a section of portraits and weddings and babies and landscape and fashion. You should just focus on the genre or genres that you are most passionate about. If you have a genre that you love that is weaker than the others, I believe that you should constantly be working to improve yourself. However you should also play to your strengths, and if you know for example, that your noir fashion shots are great, then work to make them absolutely impressive, rather than randomly choosing to include children's lifestyle photography, which may not be your strong suit. Anyone viewing your portfolio will then instantly connect to you with your noir fashion photography and be more likely to remember you in the long run then if you have an incredibly diversified portfolio. You should spend your time Learning to push your strengths to new limits rather than learning every style that there is. In this way, your voice will become unique and strong.

You can develop an aesthetic that you will be recognized for. Once you have learned to develop this aesthetic, you want to translate that over to all of your marketing materials. Marketing is especially important for fashion photographers, because you're essentially part of the marketing community. Your business cards, leave behinds, flyers, coupons, portfolio, and website should all be unified and reflective of each other. If you have a strong brand, then designers and models who also have a strong and similar brand will be attracted to working with you, thus bringing you to build your portfolio up even more.

Print For Fashion

The fashion industry is constantly changing, so today it is possible to print a fashion spread as though it were fine art. However, I do want to make a distinction between the traditional printing method for fine art and for fashion. As you know, Fashion is just glamorous advertising, and so we find most fashion photography in print magazines, and online as opposed to hanging on a gallery wall. As such, fashion photographs are often printed large as spreads. One picture in particular may be printed horizontally so that it takes up two pages of the magazine. Because the image continues over a split, you never really want have anything important going on in the middle of the photograph. Take a look at a fashion or lifestyle magazine that you have laying around the house. What things do you notice about the layout of the photographs? For one thing because we read from top to bottom, the images are typically vertical in layout unless they take up two pages. You'll also find that the model may be pushed to one side of the frame in order to allow for graphics and lettering. The colors are bold, in contrast with the typeface used.

Because fashion photographs are largely used in magazines, they often do not have borders around them like fine art. Instead, the image extends fully across the whole page.

You'll also find that fashion photography concepts revolve around current trends or ideas of the designer. Though this is changing, Fashion photography tends to be in color because you want to see the full extent of the garment. When printed, the images are extra glossy and typically saturated.

Even if you aren't being featured in a magazine, it's probably a good idea to have your fashion images printed as though they were from a magazine. This means printing across the entirety of the page, which means you might have to change your settings in Photoshop or whatever other printing service you use before hitting send. Also experiment with different glossy papers because not all are created equal. You want to make sure that your image looks professional and high-quality, especially if you're shooting editorial or high-end fashion. You never want to print fashion on matte paper because it tamps down the colors and is not reminiscent of a magazine page.

Finally, in fashion photography it's also important to make sure that your colors are accurate to the garment. The last thing you want to do is upset your client because the color does not match that of the actual garment that they are selling.

Conclusion

My hope is, that after reading this book on fashion photography, you now have the tools you need to go out and plan your own fashion shoot. You now know the difference between fashion photography and portraiture, and you understand that there are literally thousands of styles for you to pick from. The journey now it is for you to find your voice and your niche. Don't be afraid to experiment and allow that to change and grow over time.

Remember that planning a fashion photography shoot takes a lot of time and effort. You need to be meticulous in your budget and your checklist to make sure that you can get everything you want achieved. Build yourself a strong team with a good assistant, models, stylist, hair stylist, make up artist, and seamstress. If you're clear and direct from the very beginning about what you want, you will be able to keep your team on the same page and create an outstanding product for yourself and/or your client. As you grow in your talent, more designers and models might ask to work with you, you will find it much easier to ask for who you want to work with. Collaboration is a key element of fashion photography.

You also know the tools you need to shoot both on location and in the studio. In either instance you never want to forget your toolkit in case of any emergency that might arise. Before any photo shoot, I would suggest having a toolkit checklist and a general camera equipment checklist. You might also suggest to your stylist and makeup artists that they do the same. This way you can be absolutely sure that everyone has what they need and is prepared for the shoot ahead. Retouching is something that is both controversial and necessary. You have learned about the political implications of too much retouching, what it means when you do it, and when it can be used for artistic purposes. I hope that the techniques I have included are useful and generally easy for you to pick up. The importance of a portfolio cannot be undermined, both as a print and online entity. Use the tips I have enclosed to further better your portfolio, and make sure that you keep it relevant and well branded. If you find that a print portfolio is incredibly important to you, you should either find a printer that you trust to create quality work for you, or learn how to do your own printing to the highest standards. All of this combined should make one outstanding fashion photographer. I certainly hope that something in this book has provided a new insight or a new inspiration for you. Keep styling!

www.ingramcontent.com/pod-product-compliance
Lightning Source LLC
Chambersburg PA
CBHW070749180526
45168CB00004B/1568